BIBLE BLANKS

Fill-in the Missing Words - An Interactive and Entertaining Bible Study exercise

Book 1

By Rizada

TABLE OF CONTENTS

INTRODUCTION

Dive deep into the scriptures like never before with "Bible Blanks." This unique devotional challenges readers to engage with the Word of God in an interactive and enriching way. Each page presents carefully curated verses from the Bible with crucial words missing, inviting you to fill in the gaps using your knowledge, intuition, and the guidance of the Holy Spirit.

Beyond a simple test of memory, this book is designed to enhance meditation on the scriptures, allowing readers to internalize and reflect upon the timeless truths contained within. As you journey through the pages, you'll rediscover familiar verses and encounter new insights, strengthening your bond with the sacred texts.

Perfect for individual study, group Bible studies, or as a thoughtful gift for loved ones, "Bible Blanks" offers a fresh approach to scripture engagement. Whether you're a seasoned biblical scholar or a newcomer to the faith, this book promises a transformative experience as you seek to fill not just the gaps on the page, but also the gaps in your spiritual understanding.

Embrace the challenge, deepen your faith, and let "Bible Blanks" guide you on a fulfilling journey through the Word of God.

How to Use "Bible Blanks"

1. **Begin with Prayer:** Before you start, take a moment to pray. Ask the Lord for guidance, understanding, and wisdom as you engage with His Word.

2. **Have a Bible at Hand:** Ensure you have a Bible nearby. This will be essential for understanding the context and ensuring accuracy as you fill in the gaps.

3. **Choose Your Starting Point:** While the book is structured for a progressive journey, feel free to start on any page that resonates with you.

4. **Consult Your Bible:** Look up the verse in your Bible. Read the surrounding verses to understand its context. Who is speaking? What is the situation? This will often provide clues to the missing words.

5. **Read the Verse Aloud:** Before attempting to fill in the gaps, read the poem aloud. Hearing the words can help jog your memory.

6. **Reflect and Fill in the Gaps:** After reading the entire verse in your Bible, return to the book and fill in the blanks without looking back. Trust your memory and understanding.

7. **Meditate on the Verse:** Spend some time reflecting on the meaning of the verse and its relevance to your life. What is God revealing to you through it?

8. **Journal Your Insights:** Keep a journal or notebook close. Jot down any revelations, questions, or personal reflections from your study.

9. **Share and Discuss:** If you use this book with others, share your thoughts. Different perspectives can offer richer insights.

10. **Challenge Yourself:** As you become more familiar with the process, try filling in the gaps before consulting your Bible. Test your memory and see how you do.

11. **End with Gratitude:** Conclude your study session with a prayer of thanks. Express gratitude for the insights you've gained and ask for continued wisdom in your spiritual journey.

Using "Bible Blanks" alongside your Bible offers a fulfilling and enriching experience, deepening your connection to God's Word. Enjoy this unique journey of discovery and reflection!

GENESIS

1. "In the beginning God created the
   _____ and the _____." (Genesis 1:1)

2. "Then God said, 'Let there be _____,'
   and there was _____." (Genesis 1:3)

3. "God called the light ',' and the
   darkness he called '.'" (Genesis 1:5)

4. "God said, 'Let the water under the sky
   be gathered to one place, and let
   _____ appear.'" (Genesis 1:9)

5. "So God created man in his own
   _____, in the image of God he _____
   him." (Genesis 1:27)

6. "The LORD God took the man and put him in the _____ of Eden to work it and _____ it." (Genesis 2:15)

7. "But of the tree of the knowledge of good and evil, you shall not _____ it." (Genesis 2:17)

8. "The man said, 'This is now bone of my _____ and flesh of my _____.'" (Genesis 2:23)

9. "Now the serpent was more _____ than any of the wild animals the LORD God _____ made." (Genesis 3:1)

10. "Then the LORD God said to the _____, 'What is this you have _____?'" (Genesis 3:13)

11. "To Adam he said, 'Because you listened to your _____ and ate fruit from the tree about which I commanded you, 'You must not eat from it,' _____ is cursed because of you.'" (Genesis 3:17)

12. "Cain said to Abel, '_____.' Then they were in the field, Cain attacked his brother Abel and _____ him." (Genesis 4:8)

13. "Enoch walked _____ with God; then he was no more, because God _____ him away." (Genesis 5:24)

14. "The LORD saw how great the wickedness of the human _____ had become on the earth, and that every _____ of the human heart was only evil all the time." (Genesis 6:5)

15. "Noah was a _____ man, blameless among the people of his time, and he walked _____ with God." (Genesis 6:9)

16. "For forty days the flood kept coming on the _____, and as the waters increased they _____ the ark high above the earth." (Genesis 7:17)

17. "The waters _____ steadily from the earth. At the end of the hundred and fifty days the _____ came to rest on the mountains of Ararat." (Genesis 8:3-4)

18. "Then Noah built an _____ to the LORD and, taking some of all the clean animals and clean birds, he sacrificed _____ offerings on it." (Genesis 8:20)

19. "The LORD said, '_____ again will I curse the ground because of humans, even though every _____ of the human heart is evil from childhood.'" (Genesis 8:21)

20. "From these the _____ peoples spread out into their territories by their clans within their nations, each with its own _____." (Genesis 10:5)

21. "Come, let us build ourselves a city, with a _____ that reaches to the heavens, so that we may make a _____ for ourselves." (Genesis 11:4)

22. "The LORD had said to Abram, 'Go from your _____, your people and your father's household to the land I will _____ you.'" (Genesis 12:1)

23. "Abram believed the LORD, and he
    _ _ _ _ _ _ it to him as righteousness."
    (Genesis 15:6)

24. "Then God said, 'Yes, but your wife
    Sarah will bear you a son, and you will
    call him _ _ _ _ _ _.'" (Genesis 17:19)

25. "The men turned away and went
    toward Sodom, but _ _ _ _ _ _ remained
    standing before the _ _ _ _ _ _." (Genesis
    18:22)

26. "But Lot's wife looked back, and she
    became a _ _ _ _ _ _ of salt." (Genesis
    19:26)

27. "God said to him in the dream, 'Yes, I
    know you did this with a _ _ _ _ _ _ heart,
    and so I have _ _ _ _ _ _ you from sinning
    against me.'" (Genesis 20:6)

28. "Abraham looked up and there in a thicket he saw a _ _ _ _ _ _ caught by its horns. He went over and took the ram and sacrificed it as a _ _ _ _ _ _ instead of his son." (Genesis 22:13)

29. "Isaac brought her into the tent of his mother _ _ _ _ _ _, and he married Rebekah. So she became his _ _ _ _ _ _, and he loved her." (Genesis 24:67)

30. "Jacob said to his f_ _ _ _ _ _, 'I am Esau your firstborn. I have done as you told me. Please sit up and eat some of my _ _ _ _ _ _, so that you may give me your blessing.'" (Genesis 27:19)

EXODUS

1. "Now a new king _____ over Egypt, who did not know _____." (Exodus 1:8)

2. "The daughter of Pharaoh came down to bathe at the _____, while her maidens walked beside the _____." (Exodus 2:5)

3. "And Moses said, 'I will turn aside to see this great _____, why the bush is not _____.'" (Exodus 3:3)

4. "God said to Moses, 'I AM WHO I _____; and He said, 'Thus you shall say to the sons of Israel, 'I AM has sent me to _____.'" (Exodus 3:14)

5. "But Pharaoh said, 'Who is the LORD that I should obey His voice to let Israel go? I do not know the _____, nor will I let _____ go.'" (Exodus 5:2)

6. "Then the LORD said to Moses, 'Now you shall see what I will do to _____; for under compulsion he will let them go, and under compulsion he will drive them out of his _____.'" (Exodus 6:1)

7. "Moses and Aaron did just as the LORD commanded. He lifted up the staff and struck the _____ that was in the Nile, in the sight of Pharaoh and in the sight of his servants, and all the water that was in the Nile was turned to _____." (Exodus 7:20)

8. "They did not see one another, nor did anyone rise from his _ _ _ _ _ _ for three days, but all the sons of Israel had _ _ _ _ _ _ in their dwellings." (Exodus 10:23)

9. "Now the blood shall be a sign for you on the houses where you are. And when I see the _ _ _ _ _ _, I will pass over you; and the plague shall not be on you to destroy you when I strike the land of _ _ _ _ _ _." (Exodus 12:13)

10. "And the Egyptians _ _ _ _ _ _ the people, to send them out of the land in haste, for they said, 'We will all be _ _ _ _ _ _!'" (Exodus 12:33)

11. "By day the LORD went ahead of them in a pillar of _ _ _ _ _ _ to guide them on their way and by night in a pillar of _ _ _ _ _ _ to give them light." (Exodus 13:21)

12. "Then Moses stretched out his hand over the sea; and the LORD swept the sea back by a _ _ _ _ _ _ east wind all night and turned the sea into dry land, so the waters were _ _ _ _ _ _." (Exodus 14:21)

13. "The LORD is my strength and song, and He has become my _ _ _ _ _ _ ; This is my God, and I will praise Him; My father's God, and I will _ _ _ _ _ _ Him." (Exodus 15:2)

14. "He cried out to the LORD, and the LORD showed him a _ _ _ _ _ _ . And he threw it into the waters, and the waters became _ _ _ _ _ _." (Exodus 15:25)

15. "Behold, I will rain bread from heaven for you; and the _____ shall go out and gather a day's portion every day, that I may test them, whether or not they will walk in My _____." (Exodus 16:4)

16. "You shall surely set a king over you whom the LORD your God chooses, one from among your _____ you shall set as king over yourselves; you may not put a foreigner over yourselves who is not your _____." (Exodus 17:15)

17. "Now Mount Sinai was all in smoke because the LORD _____ upon it in fire; and its smoke ascended like the smoke of a furnace, and the whole mountain _____." (Exodus 19:18)

18. "You shall have no _____ gods before
    _____." (Exodus 20:3)

19. "Remember the s_____ day, to keep it
    _____." (Exodus 20:8)

20. "Honor your father and your _____,
    that your days may be _____ in the
    land which the LORD your God gives
    you." (Exodus 20:12)

21. "You shall not make for yourself an
    idol, or any _____ of what is in heaven
    above or on the earth beneath or in the
    water under the _____." (Exodus 20:4)

22. "You shall not covet your neighbor's
    house; you shall not _____ your
    neighbor's wife or his male servant or
    his female servant or his ox or his
    donkey or anything that belongs to
    your _____." (Exodus 20:17)

23. "If you meet _____ enemy's ox or his donkey wandering away, you shall surely return it to _____." (Exodus 23:4)

24. "You shall not _____ a young goat in its mother's _____." (Exodus 23:19)

25. "Behold, I am going to send an angel before you to _____ you along the way and to bring you into the place which I have _____." (Exodus 23:20)

26. "You shall not offer the blood of My sacrifice with l_____ bread; nor is the fat of My feast to remain overnight until _____." (Exodus 23:18)

27. "The LORD said to Moses, 'Come up to Me on the _____ and remain there, and I will give you the stone tablets with the law and the commandment which I have written for their _____.'" (Exodus 24:12)

28. "You shall make a mercy _____ of pure gold, two and a half cubits long and one and a half cubits _____." (Exodus 25:17)

29. "You shall make its dishes and its pans and its jars and its _____ with which to pour drink offerings; you shall make them of pure _____." (Exodus 25:29)

30. "You shall make a veil of blue and purple and scarlet material and fine twisted linen; it shall be made with cherubim, the work of a _____." (Exodus 26:31)

LEVITICUS

1. "If his offering is a burnt sacrifice of the herd, let him offer a male without _____; he shall offer it of his own _____ will at the door of the Tabernacle of Meeting." (Leviticus 1:3)

2. "And he shall put his hand on the head of his offering, and kill it at the door of the Tabernacle of _____; and Aaron's sons, the priests, shall sprinkle the blood all around on the _____." (Leviticus 3:2)

3. "When a person sins in hearing the utterance of an _____, and is a witness, whether he has seen or known of the matter—if he does not tell it, he bears _____." (Leviticus 5:1)

4. "And the priest shall make atonement for him before the LORD, and he shall be forgiven for any one of these things that he may have done in which he _____." (Leviticus 6:7)

5. "This is the law of the burnt offering, the grain _____, the sin offering, the trespass offering, the consecrations, and the sacrifice of the _____." (Leviticus 7:37)

6. "And Moses said to Aaron, 'Go to the altar, offer _____ sin offering and your burnt offering, and make atonement for yourself and for the _____.'" (Leviticus 9:7)

7. "Then Nadab and Abihu, the sons of Aaron, each took his _____ and put fire in it, put incense on it, and offered profane fire before the LORD, which He had not _____." (Leviticus 10:1)

8. "Speak to the children of Israel, saying, 'These are the _____ which you may eat among all the _____ on the earth.'" (Leviticus 11:2)

9. "If a woman has conceived, and borne a male child, _____ she shall be unclean seven days; as in the days of her customary impurity she shall be _____." (Leviticus 12:2)

10. "Now the leper on _____ the sore is, his clothes shall be torn and his head bare; and he shall cover his _____ and cry, 'Unclean! Unclean!'" (Leviticus 13:45)

11. "He shall be _____, but the scale he shall not shave; and the priest shall isolate the one who has the scale another seven _____." (Leviticus 13:33)

12. "This shall be the _____ of the leper for the day of his _____: He shall be brought to the priest." (Leviticus 14:2)

13. "If a man has an _____ of semen, he shall wash his whole body in water, and be unclean until _____." (Leviticus 15:16)

14. "You shall not _____ the nakedness of your brother's wife; it is your brother's _____." (Leviticus 18:16)

15. "You shall _____ keep My statutes and My judgments, and shall not commit any of these _____." (Leviticus 18:26)

16. "You shall not eat _____ with the blood, nor shall you practice _____ or soothsaying." (Leviticus 19:26)

17. "You shall rise _____ the gray headed and honor the presence of an old man, and fear your _____: I am the LORD." (Leviticus 19:32)

18. "You shall not _____ any cuttings in your flesh for the dead, nor tattoo any marks on _____; I am the LORD." (Leviticus 19:28)

19. "You shall not mate _____ kinds of animals. You shall not sow your field with mixed seed. Nor shall a garment of mixed linen and wool come upon _____." (Leviticus 19:19)

20. "You shall count seven sabbaths of years for yourself, _ _ _ _ _ _ times seven years; and the time of the seven sabbaths of years shall be to you forty-nine _ _ _ _ _ _ ." (Leviticus 25:8)

21. "If your brother _ _ _ _ _ _ poor, and falls into poverty among you, then you shall help him, like a stranger or a sojourner, that he may _ _ _ _ _ _ with you." (Leviticus 25:35)

22. "You shall not make idols for yourselves; _ _ _ _ _ _ a carved image nor a sacred pillar shall you rear up for yourselves; nor shall you set up an engraved stone in your land, to bow down to _ _ _ _ _ _ ; for I am the LORD your God." (Leviticus 26:1)

23. "But if you do not obey Me, and do not observe all these commandments, and if _____ despise My statutes, or if your soul abhors My judgments, so that you do not perform all My commandments, but break My _____." (Leviticus 26:14-15)

24. "I will set My face against you, and you shall be _____ by your enemies. Those who hate you shall _____ over you, and you shall flee when no one pursues you." (Leviticus 26:17)

25. "And if by these things you are not reformed by Me, but walk contrary to Me, then I also will walk _____ to you, and I will _____ you yet seven times for your sins." (Leviticus 26:23-24)

26. "But if they confess their iniquity and the _ _ _ _ _ _ of their fathers, with their unfaithfulness in which they were unfaithful to Me, and that they also have walked _ _ _ _ _ _ to Me." (Leviticus 26:40)

27. "All the _ _ _ _ _ _ of the land shall be a jubilee for you; you shall return every man to his _ _ _ _ _ _, and you shall return every man to his family." (Leviticus 25:10)

28. "If a man _ _ _ _ _ _ to the LORD part of a field of his possession, then your valuation shall be according to the seed for it. A homer of barley seed shall be valued at fifty _ _ _ _ _ _ of silver." (Leviticus 27:16)

29. "But the firstborn of a cow, the firstborn of a sheep, or the firstborn of a goat you shall not _____; they are holy. You shall sprinkle their blood on the _____, and burn their fat as an offering made by fire for a sweet aroma to the LORD." (Leviticus 27:27)

30. "These are the _____ which the LORD commanded Moses for the children of Israel on Mount _____." (Leviticus 27:34)

NUMBERS

1. "The LORD spoke to _____, saying:
    'Take a census of all the congregation of
    the _____ of Israel.'" (Numbers 1:1-2)

2. "All who were numbered of the _____,
    by their families, were two hundred
    and _____ thousand." (Numbers 3:39)

3. "Now the LORD _____ to Moses in
    the Wilderness of _____, saying,"
    (Numbers 5:1)

4. "Speak to the children of Israel: 'When
    a _____ or woman commits any sin
    that men commit in unfaithfulness
    against the _____,'" (Numbers 5:6)

5. "Then the LORD spoke to Moses, saying, 'Speak to the _____ of Israel, and say to them: 'When either a man or woman consecrates an offering to take the vow of a _____,'" (Numbers 6:1-2)

6. "And the LORD spoke to Moses, saying: 'Make two _____ trumpets for yourself; you shall make them of _____ work; you shall use them for calling the congregation and for directing the movement of the _____.'" (Numbers 10:1-2)

7. "Now when the _____ complained, it displeased the LORD; for the LORD heard it, and His anger was _____; so the fire of the LORD burned among them, and consumed some in the outskirts of the _____." (Numbers 11:1)

8. "So Moses said to the LORD, 'Why have You _____ Your servant? And why have I not found favor in Your sight, that You have laid the burden of all these _____ on me?'" (Numbers 11:11)

9. "Now the man _____was very humble, more than all men who were on the _____." (Numbers 12:3)

10. "And the LORD spoke to Moses and Aaron, saying, 'How long shall I bear with this evil congregation who complain against _____? I have heard the _____ which the children of Israel make against Me.'" (Numbers 14:26-27)

11. "But if the LORD creates a new thing, and the _____ opens its mouth and swallows them up with all that belongs to them, and they go down alive into the _____, then you will understand that these men have rejected the LORD." (Numbers 16:30)

12. "Speak to the _____ of Israel, and get from them a rod from each father's house, all their leaders according to their fathers' houses—twelve rods. Write each man's name on his _____." (Numbers 17:2)

13. "This shall be a statute forever for you: In the _____ month, on the tenth day of the month, you shall afflict your souls, and do no work at all, whether a native of your own country or a stranger who _____ among you." (Numbers 29:7)

14. "Then the LORD said to Moses: 'Get up
   into this mountain of Abarim, and see
   the _____ which I have _____ to the
   children of Israel.'" (Numbers 27:12)

15. "These are the commandments and the
   judgments _____ the LORD
   commanded the children of Israel by
   the hand of _____ in the plains of
   Moab by the Jordan, across from
   Jericho." (Numbers 36:13)

16. "And the LORD spoke to Moses,
   saying: 'Command the children of
   Israel, and _____ to them, 'My
   offering, My food for My offerings
   made by fire as a sweet aroma to Me,
   you shall be careful to offer to Me at
   their _____ time.'" (Numbers 28:1-2)

17. "And in the _____ of your months you shall offer a burnt offering to the LORD: two young bulls, one ram, and seven lambs in their first _____, without blemish." (Numbers 28:11)

18. "Also in the day of the firstfruits, when you _____ a new grain offering to the LORD at your Feast of Weeks, you shall have a holy _____. You shall do no customary work." (Numbers 28:26)

19. "These you shall present to the LORD at your appointed feasts (besides your vowed _____ and your freewill offerings) as your burnt offerings and your grain offerings, as your drink offerings and your _____ offerings." (Numbers 29:39)

20. "Then the LORD spoke to Moses, saying: 'Speak to the _ _ _ _ _ _ of Israel, saying: 'If a man dies and has no son, then you shall cause his inheritance to pass to his _ _ _ _ _ _.'" (Numbers 27:6-7)

21. "So the LORD's anger was aroused against Israel, and He _ _ _ _ _ _ them wander in the wilderness forty years, until all the generation that had done evil in the sight of the LORD was _ _ _ _ _ _." (Numbers 32:13)

22. "These are the journeys of the children of Israel, _ _ _ _ _ _ went out of the land of Egypt by their armies under the hand of _ _ _ _ _ _ and Aaron." (Numbers 33:1)

23. "But if you do not drive out the inhabitants of the _____ from before you, then it shall be that those whom you let remain shall be irritants in your eyes and thorns in your _____, and they shall harass you in the land where you dwell." (Numbers 33:55)

24. "Command the children of Israel, and say to them: '_____ you come into the land of Canaan, this is the land that shall fall to you as an _____—the land of Canaan to its boundaries." (Numbers 34:2)

25. "These are the ones the LORD commanded to divide the inheritance to the children of _____ in the land of Canaan: Eleazar the priest, Joshua the son of Nun, and the heads of the fathers of the tribes of the children of _____." (Numbers 34:29)

26. "The daughters of Zelophehad speak what is right; you _____ surely give them a possession of an inheritance among their father's brothers, and cause the inheritance of their father to pass to _____." (Numbers 27:7)

27. "And the LORD _____ to Moses: 'Take Joshua the son of Nun with you, a man in whom is the Spirit, and lay your hand on _____.'" (Numbers 27:18)

28. "Then the LORD spoke to Moses, saying: 'Speak to the children of Israel, and say to _____: 'When you have crossed the Jordan into the land of Canaan, then you shall drive out all the inhabitants of the land from before you, destroy all their engraved stones, destroy all their molded images, and demolish all their _____.'" (Numbers 33:50-52)

29. "But if you do not drive out the inhabitants of the land from before you, then it shall be _____ those whom you let remain shall be irritants in your eyes and thorns in your sides, and they shall harass you in the land where you _____." (Numbers 33:55)

30. "These are the names of the men who shall divide the _____ among you as an inheritance: Eleazar the priest and Joshua the son of _____." (Numbers 34:17)

DEUTERONOMY

1. "These are the _ _ _ _ _ _ which Moses spoke to all Israel on this side of the _ _ _ _ _ _, in the wilderness, in the plain opposite _ _ _ _ _ _." (Deuteronomy 1:1)

2. "The LORD our God _ _ _ _ _ _ to us in _ _ _ _ _ _, saying: 'You have dwelt long enough at this _ _ _ _ _ _.'" (Deuteronomy 1:6)

3. "So I spoke to you; _ _ _ _ _ _ you would not listen, and rebelled against the command of the _ _ _ _ _ _, and presumptuously went up into the _ _ _ _ _ _." (Deuteronomy 1:43)

4. "Hear, O Israel: The LORD our God, the LORD is _ _ _ _ _ _. You shall love the LORD your God with all your heart, with all your soul, and with all your _ _ _ _ _ _." (Deuteronomy 6:4-5)

5. "When your son asks you in time to come, saying, 'What is the _____ of the testimonies, the statutes, and the judgments which the LORD our God has _____ us?'" (Deuteronomy 6:20)

6. "For if you carefully keep all these _____ which I command you to do— to love the LORD your God, to walk in all His ways, and to hold fast to _____," (Deuteronomy 11:22)

7. "You shall not eat it, that it may go well with _____ and your children after you, when you do what is right in the _____ of the LORD." (Deuteronomy 12:25)

8. "If your brother, the son of your mother, your son or your daughter, the wife of your _____, or your friend who is as your own soul, secretly entices you, saying, 'Let us go and serve other _____,' which you have not known, neither you nor your fathers," (Deuteronomy 13:6)

9. "You shall not _____ interest to your brother—interest on money or food or anything that is _____ for interest." (Deuteronomy 23:19)

10. "When you make a vow to the LORD your God, you _____ not delay to pay it; for the LORD your God will surely require it of you, and it would be _____ to you." (Deuteronomy 23:21)

11. "When you come _____ your neighbor's vineyard, you may eat your fill of grapes at your pleasure, but you shall not put any in your _____." (Deuteronomy 23:24)

12. "If there is among you a poor man of your brethren, _____ any of the gates in your land which the LORD your God is giving you, you shall not harden your heart nor shut your hand from your _____ brother." (Deuteronomy 15:7)

13. "You shall _____ that you were a slave in the land of _____, and the LORD your God redeemed you; therefore I command you this thing today." (Deuteronomy 15:15)

14. "Three times a year all your males shall appear _____ the LORD your God in the place which He chooses: at the Feast of Unleavened Bread, at the Feast of Weeks, and at the Feast of _____." (Deuteronomy 16:16)

15. "You shall not _____ justice; you shall not show partiality, nor take a _____, for a bribe blinds the eyes of the wise and twists the words of the righteous." (Deuteronomy 16:19)

16. "If a false _____ rises against any man to testify against him of _____," (Deuteronomy 19:16)

17. "Your eye shall not _____ him, but you shall purge the guilt of innocent _____ from Israel, that it may go well with you." (Deuteronomy 19:13)

18. "When you _____ a city for a long time, while making war against it to take it, you shall not destroy its trees by wielding an ax against them; if you can eat of them, do not cut them down to use in the _____, for the tree of the field is man's food." (Deuteronomy 20:19)

19. "If a man has _____ a sin deserving of death, and he is put to death, and you hang him on a _____," (Deuteronomy 21:22)

20. "When you build a _____ house, then you shall make a parapet for your roof, that you may not bring guilt of _____ on your household if anyone falls from it." (Deuteronomy 22:8)

21. "You shall not see your brother's ox or his sheep going _____, and hide yourself from them; you shall certainly bring them back to your _____."
(Deuteronomy 22:1)

22. "If a man is found _____ with a woman married to a husband, then both of them shall die—the man that lay with the woman, and the _____; so you shall put away the evil from Israel."
(Deuteronomy 22:22)

23. "When you reap your harvest in your field, and forget a _____ in the field, you shall not go back to get it; it shall be for the stranger, the fatherless, and the widow, that the LORD your God may _____ you in all the work of your hands." (Deuteronomy 24:19)

24. "Cursed is the _ _ _ _ _ _ who treats his father or his mother with _ _ _ _ _ _!' And all the people shall say, 'Amen!'" (Deuteronomy 27:16)

25. "The LORD will cause you to be defeated before your _ _ _ _ _ _; you shall go out one way against them and flee seven ways before them; and you shall become troublesome to all the _ _ _ _ _ _ of the earth." (Deuteronomy 28:25)

26. "In the morning you shall say, 'Oh, that it were evening!' And at _ _ _ _ _ _ you shall say, 'Oh, that it were morning!' because of the fear which terrifies your heart, and because of the sight which your _ _ _ _ _ _ see." (Deuteronomy 28:67)

27. "Then Moses called Joshua and said to him in the sight of all Israel, 'Be strong and of good _____, for you must go with this people to the land which the LORD has sworn to their fathers to give them, and you shall cause them to _____ it.'" (Deuteronomy 31:7)

28. "Give ear, O heavens, and I _____ speak; And hear, O earth, the words of my _____." (Deuteronomy 32:1)

29. "For I proclaim the _____ of the LORD: Ascribe greatness to our _____!" (Deuteronomy 32:3)

30. "Then Moses _____ up from the plains of Moab to Mount Nebo, to the top of Pisgah, which is across from _____." (Deuteronomy 34:1)

JOSHUA

1. "After the death of _____ the servant
   of the LORD, it came to pass that the
   LORD spoke to Joshua the son of Nun,
   Moses' _____, saying," (Joshua 1:1)

2. "Every place that the _____ of your
   foot will tread upon I have _____ to
   you, as I said to Moses." (Joshua 1:3)

3. "Only be strong and very _____ , that
   you may observe to do according to all
   the law which Moses My servant
   _____ you; do not turn from it to the
   right hand or to the left, that you may
   prosper wherever you go." (Joshua 1:7)

4. "And they answered _____ , saying, 'All that you command us we will do, and wherever you send us we will _____.'" (Joshua 1:16)

5. "Then Joshua the son of _____ sent two men as spies secretly from Shittim, saying, 'Go, view the land, especially _____.'" (Joshua 2:1)

6. "And she said to the men: 'I know that the LORD has given you the land, that the _____ of you has fallen on us, and that all the inhabitants of the land are _____ because of you.'" (Joshua 2:9)

7. "So the men said to her: 'Our life for yours, if _____ of you tell this business of ours. And it shall be, when the LORD has given us the land, that we will deal kindly and _____ with you.'" (Joshua 2:14)

8. "Then you shall return to the land of your _____ and enjoy it, which Moses the LORD's servant gave you on the _____ side of the Jordan." (Joshua 1:15)

9. "And it shall come to pass, as soon as the soles of the _____ of the priests who bear the ark of the LORD, the Lord of all the earth, shall rest in the waters of the Jordan, that the waters of the Jordan shall be _____, the waters that come down from upstream, and they shall stand as a heap." (Joshua 3:13)

10. "On that day the LORD exalted Joshua in the _____ of all Israel; and they feared him, as they had feared Moses, all the days of his _____." (Joshua 4:14)

11. "Then the LORD said to Joshua, 'This day I have rolled _____ the reproach of Egypt from you.' Therefore the name of the place is called _____ to this day." (Joshua 5:9)

12. "And the commander of the LORD's _____ said to Joshua, 'Take your sandal off your foot, for the place where you stand is _____.' And Joshua did so." (Joshua 5:15)

13. "Now Jericho was securely shut up _____ of the children of Israel; none went out, and none came _____." (Joshua 6:1)

14. "You shall march _____ the city, all you men of war; you shall go all around the city once. This you shall do _____ days." (Joshua 6:3)

15. "So the people shouted when the priests blew the _ _ _ _ _ _ . And it happened when the people heard the sound of the trumpet, and the people shouted with a great shout, that the wall _ _ _ _ _ _ down flat." (Joshua 6:20)

16. "But the children of Israel committed a trespass regarding the accursed things, for _ _ _ _ _ _ the son of Carmi, the son of Zabdi, the son of Zerah, of the tribe of Judah, took of the accursed things; so the anger of the LORD burned against the children of _ _ _ _ _ _." (Joshua 7:1)

17. "O Lord, what shall I say when _ _ _ _ _ _ turns its back before its _ _ _ _ _ _?" (Joshua 7:8)

18. "So about _ _ _ _ _ _ thousand men went up there from the people, but they fled before the men of _ _ _ _ _ _." (Joshua 7:4)

19. "Now Joshua sent men from Jericho to Ai, which is _ _ _ _ _ _ Beth Aven, on the east side of Bethel, and spoke to them, saying, 'Go up and spy out the _ _ _ _ _ _!' So the men went up and spied out Ai." (Joshua 7:2)

20. "And the LORD said to Joshua: 'Do not be afraid, nor be _ _ _ _ _ _ ; take all the people of war with you, and arise, go up to Ai. See, I have given into your hand the king of Ai, his people, his city, and his _ _ _ _ _ _.'" (Joshua 8:1)

21. "Then the LORD said to Joshua, 'Stretch out the spear that is in your hand toward _____ , for I will give it into your hand.' And Joshua stretched out the spear that was in his hand toward the _____." (Joshua 8:18)

22. "So Joshua made a _____ with the people that day, and made for them a statute and an ordinance in _____." (Joshua 24:25)

23. "And the men of Gibeon sent to Joshua at the camp at Gilgal, saying, 'Do not _____ your servants; come up to us quickly, save us and help us, for all the kings of the Amorites who dwell in the mountains have gathered together against _____.'" (Joshua 10:6)

24. "Then Joshua spoke to the LORD in the day when the LORD delivered up the _____ before the children of Israel, and he said in the sight of Israel: 'Sun, stand still over _____, and Moon, in the Valley of Aijalon.'" (Joshua 10:12)

25. "And at that time Joshua came and cut off the _____ from the mountains: from Hebron, from Debir, from Anab, from all the mountains of Judah, and from all the mountains of _____; Joshua utterly destroyed them with their cities." (Joshua 11:21)

26. "These are the areas which Moses had distributed as an _____ in the plains of Moab on the other side of the Jordan, by Jericho _____." (Joshua 13:32)

27. "The lot for the tribe of the children of Judah _____ to their families was to the boundary of Edom, to the Wilderness of _____ southward." (Joshua 15:1)

28. "And to Caleb the son of Jephunneh he gave a part among the _____ of Judah, according to the commandment of the LORD to Joshua, namely, Kirjath Arba, which is _____ (Arba was the father of Anak)." (Joshua 15:13)

29. "Now the cities of the tribe of the children of _____, according to their families, were Jericho, Beth Hoglah, Emek Keziz," (Joshua 18:21)

30. "So the LORD gave to Israel all the land of which He had _____ to give to their fathers, and they took possession of it and _____ in it." (Joshua 21:43)

JUDGES

1. "After the death of Joshua, the children of Israel _____ the LORD, saying, 'Who shall go up for us against the Canaanites first to fight against _____?'" (Judges 1:1)

2. "But the children of Benjamin did not drive out the J_____ who inhabited Jerusalem; so the Jebusites dwell with the children of Benjamin in Jerusalem to this _____." (Judges 1:21)

3. "And the Angel of the LORD came up from Gilgal to _____ , and said: 'I led you up from Egypt and brought you to the land of which I swore to your fathers; and I said, "I will never break My _____ with you."'" (Judges 2:1)

4. "When the LORD raised up judges for them, the LORD was with the judge and _____ them out of the hand of their enemies all the days of the _____." (Judges 2:18)

5. "Then the children of _____ did evil in the sight of the LORD, and served the _____." (Judges 2:11)

6. "So the _____ of the LORD was hot against Israel; and He said, 'Because this nation has transgressed My covenant which I_____ their fathers, and has not heeded My voice, I also will no longer drive out before them any of the nations which Joshua left when he _____.'" (Judges 2:20-21)

7. "And they would not listen to their judges, but they _____ the harlot with other gods, and bowed down to _____. They turned quickly from the way in which their fathers walked, in _____ the commandments of the LORD; they did not do so." (Judges 2:17)

8. "Now Deborah, a _____ the wife of Lapidoth, was judging Israel at that _____." (Judges 4:4)

9. "And she sent and called for Barak the son of _____ from Kedesh in Naphtali, and said to him, 'Has not the LORD God of Israel commanded, "Go and deploy troops at Mount Tabor; take with you ten thousand men of the sons of Naphtali and of the sons of _____?"'" (Judges 4:6)

10. "Then Deborah said to _____ , 'Up! For this is the day in which the LORD has delivered Sisera into your hand. Has not the LORD gone out before _____?'" (Judges 4:14)

11. "Then the _____ had rest for _____ years." (Judges 5:31)

12. "So the children of Israel did _____ in the sight of the LORD. They forgot the LORD their God, and served the _____ and the Ashtoreths." (Judges 3:7)

13. "Then the children of Israel cried out to the LORD, and the LORD raised up a _____ for the children of Israel, who delivered them: Othniel the son of Kenaz, Caleb's _____ brother." (Judges 3:9)

14. "And the Spirit of the LORD came upon him, and he _____ Israel. He went out to war, and the LORD delivered Cushan-Rishathaim king of Mesopotamia into his hand; and his hand _____ against Cushan-Rishathaim." (Judges 3:10)

15. "Then the children of Israel again did evil in the sight of the LORD, and served the Baals and the _____ , the gods of Syria, the gods of Sidon, the gods of Moab, the gods of the people of Ammon, and the gods of the _____." (Judges 10:6)

16. "And the LORD said to the children of Israel, 'Did I not _____ you from the Egyptians and from the Amorites and from the people of Ammon and from the _____?'" (Judges 10:11)

17. "Then the Spirit of the LORD came upon Jephthah, and he _____ through Gilead and Manasseh, and passed through Mizpah of Gilead; and from Mizpah of Gilead he advanced toward the people of _____." (Judges 11:29)

18. "And Jephthah made a vow to the LORD, and said, 'If You will _____ deliver the people of Ammon into my hands, then it will be that whatever comes out of the _____ of my house to meet me, when I return in peace from the people of Ammon, shall surely be the LORD's, and I will offer it up as a _____ offering.'" (Judges 11:30-31)

19. "And the men of _____ gathered together, crossed over toward Zaphon, and said to _____ , 'Why did you cross over to fight against the people of Ammon, and did not call us to go with _____? We will burn your house down on you with fire!'" (Judges 12:1)

20. "After him, _____ of Bethlehem judged _____." (Judges 12:8)

21. "Now the Angel of the LORD came up from _____ to Bochim, and said: 'I led you up from Egypt and brought you to the land of which I swore to your fathers; and I said, "I will never break My covenant with _____."'" (Judges 2:1)

22. "And the children of Israel did evil again in the _ _ _ _ _ _ of the LORD, and served the Baals and the Ashtoreths, the gods of Syria, the gods of Sidon, the gods of Moab, the gods of the people of Ammon, and the gods of the _ _ _ _ _ _." (Judges 10:6)

23. "Then Samson said, 'With the jawbone of a _ _ _ _ _ _. heaps upon heaps, with the jawbone of a donkey I have _ _ _ _ _ _ a thousand men!'" (Judges 15:16)

24. "So Delilah said to _ _ _ _ _ _ , 'Please tell me where your great strength lies, and with what you may be _ _ _ _ _ _ to afflict you.'" (Judges 16:6)

25. "Then the _ _ _ _ _ _ took him and put out his eyes, and brought him down to Gaza. They bound him with bronze fetters, and he became a grinder in the _ _ _ _ _ _." (Judges 16:21)

26. "And Samson said, 'Let me die with the
    _____!' And he pushed with all his
    might, and the _____ fell on the lords
    and all the people who were in it."
    (Judges 16:30)

27. "In those days there was no _____ in
    Israel; everyone did what was right in
    his own _____." (Judges 17:6)

28. "And the children of _____ set up for
    themselves the carved image; and
    _____ the son of Gershom, the son of
    Manasseh, and his sons were priests to
    the tribe of Dan until the day of the
    captivity of the _____." (Judges 18:30)

29. "In those days there was no _____ in Israel. And in those days the tribe of the Danites was _____ an inheritance for itself to dwell in; for until that day their inheritance among the tribes of Israel had not ___'___ to them." (Judges 18:1)

30. "And the children of Benjamin did not drive out the _____ who inhabited Jerusalem; so the Jebusites dwell with the children of Benjamin in Jerusalem to this _____." (Judges 1:21)

RUTH

1. "In the days when the judges ruled, there was a _____ in the land, and a man from Bethlehem in Judah, together with his wife and two sons, went to live for a while in the country of _____." (Ruth 1:1)

2. "The man's name was _____ , his wife's name was Naomi, and the names of his two sons were Mahlon and _____, Ephrathites from Bethlehem, Judah." (Ruth 1:2)

3. "After they had _____ there about ten years, both Mahlon and Kilion also died, and Naomi was left without her two sons and her _____." (Ruth 1:5)

4. "When Naomi heard in Moab that the LORD had _____ to the aid of his people by providing food for them, she and her daughters-in-law prepared to return _____ from there." (Ruth 1:6)

5. "But _____ replied, 'Don't urge me to leave you or to turn back from you. Where you go I will go, and where you stay I will _____.'" (Ruth 1:16)

6. "So _____ returned from Moab accompanied by Ruth the Moabite, her daughter-in-law, arriving in Bethlehem as the _____ was beginning." (Ruth 1:22)

7. "Now Naomi had a _____ on her husband's side, a man of standing from the clan of Elimelek, whose name was _____." (Ruth 2:1)

8. "So Ruth went out, entered a field and began to glean _____ the harvesters. As it turned out, she was working in a field belonging to _____, who was from the clan of Elimelek." (Ruth 2:3)

9. "Boaz asked the _____ of his harvesters, 'Who does that young woman _____ to?'" (Ruth 2:5)

10. "At mealtime _____ said to her, 'Come over here. Have some bread and dip it in the _____.'" (Ruth 2:14)

11. "She carried it _____ to town, and her mother-in-law saw how much she had gathered. Ruth also brought out and gave her what she had _____ after she had eaten enough." (Ruth 2:18)

12. "Naomi said to Ruth her daughter-in-law, 'It will be good for you, my daughter, to go with the _____ who work for him, because in someone else's field you might be _____.'" (Ruth 2:22)

13. "One day Ruth's mother-in-law Naomi said to her, 'My _____ , I must find a home for you, where you will be well _____.'" (Ruth 3:1)

14. "So she went _____ to the threshing floor and did everything her mother-in-law told her to _____." (Ruth 3:6)

15. "In the middle of the _____ something startled the man; he turned—and there was a woman lying at his _____!" (Ruth 3:8)

16. "He said, 'Who are you?' And she answered, 'I am Ruth, your servant. Spread the corner of your garment over me, for you are a _____.'" (Ruth 3:9)

17. "Boaz said, 'The LORD bless you, my daughter. This _____ is greater than that which you showed earlier: You have not run after the younger men, whether rich or _____.'" (Ruth 3:10)

18. "Boaz said, 'On the _____ you buy the land from Naomi, you also acquire Ruth the Moabite, the dead man's _____.'" (Ruth 4:5)

19. "Then Boaz _____ to the elders and all the people, 'Today you are witnesses that I have bought from Naomi all the property of Elimelek, Kilion and _____.'" (Ruth 4:9)

20. "So Boaz took Ruth and she became his wife. When he _ _ _ _ _ _ love to her, the LORD enabled her to _ _ _ _ _ _, and she gave birth to a son." (Ruth 4:13)

21. "The women said to _ _ _ _ _ _ : 'Praise be to the LORD, who this day has not left you without a _ _ _ _ _ _.'" (Ruth 4:14)

22. "Then Naomi _ _ _ _ _ _ the child in her arms and cared for him. The women living there said, 'Naomi has a son!' And they named him Obed. He was the father of Jesse, the father of _ _ _ _ _ _." (Ruth 4:16-17)

23. "The name of the man was _ _ _ _ _ _ and the name of his wife Naomi, and the names of his two sons were Mahlon and Kilion. They were Ephrathites from _ _ _ _ _ _, Judah." (Ruth 1:2)

24. "She said to them, 'Do not call me
    Naomi; call me _ _ _ _ _ _ , for the
    Almighty has dealt very _ _ _ _ _ _ with
    me.'" (Ruth 1:20)

25. "So she set out from the place where
    she was with her _ _ _ _ _ _ daughters-in-
    law and they went on the way to return
    to the land of _ _ _ _ _ _." (Ruth 1:7)

26. "Then she left, and went and _ _ _ _ _ _ in
    the field after the reapers. And she
    happened to come to the part of the
    field belonging to Boaz, who was of the
    family of _ _ _ _ _ _." (Ruth 2:3)

27. "Then she said, '_ _ _ _ _ _ let me glean and
    gather after the reapers among the
    _ _ _ _ _ _.'" (Ruth 2:7)

28. "And at _____ Boaz said to her, 'Come here and eat some bread, and dip your morsel in the _____.'" (Ruth 2:14)

29. "And when she _____ up to glean, Boaz commanded his young men, saying, 'Let her glean even among the sheaves, and do not _____ her.'" (Ruth 2:15)

30. "And she took it up and went into the city. Her _____ saw what she had gleaned, and she brought out and gave what she had _____ after being satisfied." (Ruth 2:18)

1 SAMUEL

1. "Now there was a certain man of
   Ramathaim _____ of the mountains
   of Ephraim, and his name was Elkanah
   the son of Jeroham, the son of Elihu,
   the son of Tohu, the son of Zuph, an
   _____." (1 Samuel 1:1)

2. "But to Hannah he would _____ a
   double portion, for he loved Hannah,
   although the LORD had _____ her
   womb." (1 Samuel 1:5)

3. "And she was in _____ of soul, and
   prayed to the LORD and wept _____."
   (1 Samuel 1:10)

4. "Then _____ answered and said, 'Go
   in peace, and the God of Israel grant
   your _____ that you have asked of
   Him.'" (1 Samuel 1:17)

5. "For this_____ I prayed, and the LORD has granted me my _____ which I asked of Him." (1 Samuel 1:27)

6. "The bows of the _____ men are broken, and those who stumbled are girded with _____." (1 Samuel 2:4)

7. "Then a man of _____ came to Eli and said to him, 'Thus says the LORD: "Did I not clearly reveal myself to the house of your father when they were in Egypt in Pharaoh's _____?"'" (1 Samuel 2:27)

8. "And the child _____ grew before the LORD, while Eli was growing _____ in his eyes." (1 Samuel 3:2)

9. "Then the LORD called _____ , and he answered, '_____ am I.'" (1 Samuel 3:4)

10. "Then the LORD said to Samuel, 'Behold, I will do _____ in Israel at which both ears of everyone who hears it will _____.'" (1 Samuel 3:11)

11. "So the Philistines _____ , and Israel was defeated, and every man fled to his tent. There was a very great slaughter, and there fell of Israel thirty thousand _____." (1 Samuel 4:10)

12. "Then the _____ took the ark of God and brought it from Ebenezer to _____." (1 Samuel 4:11)

13. "Then the men of Beth _____ said, 'Who is able to stand before this holy LORD God? And to whom shall it go up from _____?'" (1 Samuel 6:20)

14. "So they sent messengers to the inhabitants of Kirjath Jearim, saying, 'The Philistines have _____ back the ark of the LORD; come down and take it up to _____.'" (1 Samuel 6:21)

15. "Then all the _____ of Israel gathered together and came to Samuel at _____." (1 Samuel 8:4)

16. "But the thing _____ Samuel when they said, 'Give us a king to _____ us.' So Samuel prayed to the LORD." (1 Samuel 8:6)

17. "And the LORD said to Samuel, 'Heed the voice of the _____ in all that they say to you; for they have not rejected you, but they have rejected Me, that I should not reign _____ them.'" (1 Samuel 8:7)

18. "Now there was a _ _ _ _ _ _ of Benjamin, whose name was Kish the son of Abiel, the son of Zeror, the son of Bechorath, the son of Aphiah, a Benjamite, a _ _ _ _ _ _ of power." (1 Samuel 9:1)

19. "Then Samuel took a flask of oil and poured it on his _ _ _ _ _ _ , and kissed him and said: 'Is it not because the LORD has anointed you commander over His _ _ _ _ _ _, Israel?'" (1 Samuel 10:1)

20. "Then Samuel said to the _ _ _ _ _ _ , 'Come, let us go to Gilgal and renew the _ _ _ _ _ _ there.'" (1 Samuel 11:14)

21. "Samuel also said to _ _ _ _ _ _ , 'The LORD sent me to anoint you king over His people, over Israel. Now therefore, heed the voice of the words of the _ _ _ _ _ _.'" (1 Samuel 15:1)

22. "But Samuel said, '_____ then is this bleating of the sheep in my ears, and the lowing of the _____ which I hear?'" (1 Samuel 15:14)

23. "_____ Samuel said to him, 'The LORD has torn the kingdom of Israel from you today, and has given it to a neighbor of yours, who is _____ than you.'" (1 Samuel 15:28)

24. "So it came to pass, when the evil spirit from God was _____ Saul, that David would take a harp and play it with his hand. Then Saul would become refreshed and well, and the evil spirit would _____ from him." (1 Samuel 16:23)

25. "Then David _____ to the men who stood by him, saying, 'What shall be done for the man who kills this Philistine and takes away the reproach from Israel? For who is this uncircumcised Philistine, that he should defy the _____ of the living God?'" (1 Samuel 17:26)

26. "And Saul said to David, 'You are not able to go against this _____ to fight with him; for you are a youth, and he a man of _____ from his youth.'" (1 Samuel 17:33)

27. "Then David said to the Philistine, 'You come to me with a _____ , with a spear, and with a javelin. But I come to you in the name of the LORD of hosts, the God of the armies of Israel, whom you have _____.'" (1 Samuel 17:45)

28. "Now when he had _____ speaking to Saul, the soul of Jonathan was knit to the soul of David, and Jonathan _____ him as his own soul." (1 Samuel 18:1)

29. "Then Saul was very _____ , and the saying displeased him; and he said, 'They have ascribed to David ten thousands, and to me they have ascribed only thousands. Now what more can he have but the _____?'" (1 Samuel 18:8)

30. "And Saul spoke to _____ his son and to all his servants, that they should kill _____. But Jonathan, Saul's son, delighted greatly in David." (1 Samuel 19:1)

2 SAMUEL

1. "After the death of Saul, when David had _____ from striking down the Amalekites, David remained two days in _____." (2 Samuel 1:1)

2. "David took up this _____ concerning Saul and his son _____." (2 Samuel 1:17)

3. "Then all the tribes of _____ came to David at Hebron and said, 'Behold, we are your _____ and flesh.'" (2 Samuel 5:1)

4. "And David _____ greater and greater, for the LORD, the God of hosts, was _____ him." (2 Samuel 5:10)

5. "And David danced before the LORD with all his _____ . And David was wearing a linen _____." (2 Samuel 6:14)

6. "And the king _____ to Nathan the prophet, 'See now, I dwell in a house of cedar, but the ark of God dwells in a _____.'" (2 Samuel 7:2)

7. "Your house and _____ kingdom shall be made sure forever before me. Your throne shall be established _____." (2 Samuel 7:16)

8. "And David said on that _____ , 'Whoever would strike the Jebusites, let him get up the water shaft to attack 'the lame and the blind,' who are hated by _____ soul.'" (2 Samuel 5:8)

9. "Then David _____ his wife, Bathsheba, and went in to her and lay with her, and she bore a son, and he called his name _____." (2 Samuel 12:24)

10. "Now Absalom, David's _____ , had a beautiful sister, whose name was _____. And after a time Amnon, David's son, loved her." (2 Samuel 13:1)

11. "But Absalom _____ and went to Talmai the son of Ammihud, king of _____." (2 Samuel 13:37)

12. "And the _____ said, 'And where is your master's son?' Ziba said to the king, 'Behold, he _____ at Jerusalem, for he said, 'Today the house of Israel will give me back the kingdom of my _____.'''" (2 Samuel 16:3)

13. "And the king said to Zadok, 'Carry the ark of God back into the city. If I find favor in the _ _ _ _ _ _ of the LORD, he will bring me back and let me see both it and his _ _ _ _ _ _ place.'" (2 Samuel 15:25)

14. "And _ _ _ _ _ _ said to Absalom, 'No, for whom the LORD and this people and all the men of Israel have chosen, his will I be, and with him will I _ _ _ _ _ _.'" (2 Samuel 16:18)

15. "And _ _ _ _ _ _ came to Mahanaim. And Absalom crossed the Jordan with all the men of _ _ _ _ _ _." (2 Samuel 17:24)

16. "Now Absalom _____ to meet the servants of David. Absalom was riding on his mule, and the mule went under the thick _____ of a great oak, and his head caught fast in the oak, and he was suspended between _____ and earth, while the mule that was under him went on." (2 Samuel 18:9)

17. "Then the _____ arrived and said, 'Good news, my lord the king! For the LORD has delivered you this day from all who rose up against _____.'" (2 Samuel 18:31)

18. "And the _____ said to his servants, 'Do you not know that a prince and a great man has fallen this day in _____?'" (2 Samuel 3:38)

19. "And Joab said to the king, 'Now may the LORD your _____ add to the people a hundred times as many as they are, while the _____ of my lord the king still see it, but why does my lord the king delight in this _____?'" (2 Samuel 24:3)

20. "So the king called the _____ and spoke to them. Now the Gibeonites were not of the people of Israel but of the remnant of the _____ . Although the people of Israel had sworn to spare them, Saul had sought to strike them down in his zeal for the people of _____." (2 Samuel 21:2)

21. "David said to him, 'Your blood be on your head, for your own mouth has testified against you, saying, 'I have killed the LORD's _____.'"" (2 Samuel 1:16)

22. "And David said to _____ and to all his servants, 'Behold, my own son seeks my life; _____ much more now may this Benjaminite! Leave him alone, and let him curse, for the LORD has told him _____.'" (2 Samuel 16:11)

23. "And the king said to _____ , 'Do all that is in your heart, for the LORD is _____ you.'" (2 Samuel 7:3)

24. "And David said to _____ , 'Go down to your house and wash your _____.'" (2 Samuel 11:8)

25. "Then David said to Nathan, 'I have sinned against the _____.' And Nathan said to David, 'The LORD also has put away your _____ ; you shall not die.'" (2 Samuel 12:13)

26. "And David said to _____ , 'To whom do you belong? And where are you from?' He said, 'I am a young man of Egypt, servant to an Amalekite, and my master left me behind because I fell _____ three days ago.'" (2 Samuel 1:13)

27. "And the _____ and his men went to Jerusalem against the Jebusites, the inhabitants of the land, who said to David, 'You will not come in here, but the blind and the lame will ward you off'—thinking, 'David cannot come in _____.'" (2 Samuel 5:6)

28. "And the king said to the _____ , 'Is it well with the young man Absalom?' And the _____ answered, 'May the enemies of my lord the king and all who rise up against you for evil be like that _____ man.'" (2 Samuel 18:32)

29. "And the king said to _____, 'Why
    have you brought these?' _____
    answered, 'The donkeys are for the
    king's household to ride on, the bread
    and summer fruit for the young men to
    eat, and the wine for those who _____
    in the wilderness to drink.'" (2 Samuel
    16:2)

30. "And _____ said to him, 'How is it
    you were not afraid to put out your
    hand to destroy the LORD's _____?'"
    (2 Samuel 1:14)

1 Kings

1. "Now King _____ was old and advanced in years. And although they covered him with clothes, he could not get _____." (1 Kings 1:1)

2. "Then Nathan said to _____ the mother of Solomon, 'Have you not heard that Adonijah the son of Haggith has become king and David our lord does not _____ it?'" (1 Kings 1:11)

3. "And Solomon said, 'If he will show himself a _____ man, not one of his hairs shall fall to the earth, but if wickedness is found in him, he shall _____.'" (1 Kings 1:52)

4. "At Gibeon the LORD appeared to Solomon in a _____ by night, and God said, 'Ask what I shall _____ you.'" (1 Kings 3:5)

5. "And the king went to _____ to sacrifice there, for that was the great high place. Solomon used to offer a thousand burnt offerings on that _____." (1 Kings 3:4)

6. "Then two _____ came to the king and stood before _____." (1 Kings 3:16)

7. "And the woman whose son was alive said to the king, because her _____ yearned for her son, 'Oh, my lord, give her the living child, and by no means _____ it.' But the other said, 'He shall be neither mine nor yours; divide it.'" (1 Kings 3:26)

8. "And all Israel heard of the judgment that the king had _____ , and they stood in awe of the king, because they perceived that the wisdom of God was in him to do _____." (1 Kings 3:28)

9. "And Hiram king of Tyre sent his servants to _____ when he heard that they had anointed him king in place of his father, for Hiram was always a _____ of David." (1 Kings 5:1)

10. "And the word of the LORD came to Solomon, '_____ this house that you are building, if you will walk in my statutes and obey my rules and keep all my _____ and walk in them, then I will establish my word with you, which I spoke to David your _____.'" (1 Kings 6:11-12)

11. "In the _____ year the foundation of the house of the LORD was laid, in the month of _____." (1 Kings 6:37)

12. "So _ _ _ _ _ _ built the house and finished it. He lined the walls of the house on the inside with boards of cedar. From the floor of the house to the walls of the _ _ _ _ _ _ , he covered them on the inside with wood, and he covered the floor of the house with boards of _ _ _ _ _ _." (1 Kings 6:14-15)

13. "And when the _ _ _ _ _ _ of Sheba heard of the fame of Solomon concerning the name of the LORD, she came to test him with _ _ _ _ _ _ questions." (1 Kings 10:1)

14. "And she gave the king 120 talents of gold, and a very great quantity of spices and _ _ _ _ _ _ stones. Never again came such an abundance of spices as these that the queen of Sheba gave to King _ _ _ _ _ _." (1 Kings 10:10)

15. "And King Solomon gave to the _____
of Sheba all that she desired, whatever
she asked besides what was given her
by the _____ of King Solomon. So she
turned and went back to her own
_____." (1 Kings 10:13)

16. "And the LORD was _____ with
Solomon, because his heart had turned
away from the LORD, the God of
Israel, who had appeared to him
_____." (1 Kings 11:9)

17. "And the LORD _____ up an
adversary against Solomon, Hadad the
Edomite. He was of the royal house in
_____." (1 Kings 11:14)

18. "Jeroboam the son of Nebat, an
Ephraimite of _____ , a servant of
Solomon, whose mother's name was
Zeruah, a widow, also lifted up his
hand against the _____." (1 Kings 11:26)

19. "And this was the reason why he lifted up his hand _____ the king. Solomon built the Millo, and closed up the breach of the city of David his _____." (1 Kings 11:27)

20. "And the man Jeroboam was very able, and when _____ saw that the young man was industrious he gave him charge over all the forced labor of the house of _____." (1 Kings 11:28)

21. "And it came to pass, when Jeroboam the son of Nebat heard of it (for he was still in _____ , where he had fled from King Solomon), that Jeroboam returned from _____." (1 Kings 12:2)

22. "And Rehoboam went to _____ , for all Israel had come to Shechem to make him _____." (1 Kings 12:1)

23. "But he abandoned the counsel that the old men _ _ _ _ _ _ him and took counsel with the young men who had grown up with him and stood before _ _ _ _ _ _." (1 Kings 12:8)

24. "And when all Israel saw that the king did _ _ _ _ _ _ listen to them, the people answered the king, 'What _ _ _ _ _ _ do we have in David? We have no inheritance in the son of Jesse. To your tents, O Israel! Look now to your own house, David.' So Israel went to their _ _ _ _ _ _." (1 Kings 12:16)

25. "And when the _ _ _ _ _ _ who had brought him back from the way heard of it, he said, 'It is the _ _ _ _ _ _ of God who disobeyed the word of the LORD; therefore the LORD has given him to the lion, which has torn him and killed him, according to the word that the LORD spoke to _ _ _ _ _ _.'" (1 Kings 13:26)

26. "And behold, a man of God came out of Judah by the _____ of the LORD to Bethel. Jeroboam was standing by the altar to make _____." (1 Kings 13:1)

27. "And as soon as he had finished offering the burnt _____ Jehu said to the guard and to the officers, 'Go in and strike them down; let not a man _____.' And they struck them down with the edge of the sword, and the guard and the officers cast them out and went into the inner room of the house of Baal." (1 Kings 10:25)

28. "And they _____ after them as far as the Jordan, and behold, all the way was littered with _____ and equipment that the Syrians had thrown away in their haste. And the messengers returned and told the _____." (1 Kings 7:15)

29. "And the king of Israel said to Jehoshaphat, 'There is yet one man by whom we may inquire of the LORD, Micaiah the son of _____ but I hate him, for he never prophesies good concerning me, but _____.'" (1 Kings 22:8)

30. "And _____ said, '_____ , you shall

2 KINGS

1. "Now after the _____ of Ahab, Moab rebelled against _____." (2 Kings 1:1)

2. "Then he went up from there to Bethel; and as he was _____ up the road, some youths came out of the city and mocked him, and said to him, 'Go up, you baldhead! Go _____!'" (2 Kings 2:23)

3. "So he went and did _____ to the word of the LORD, for he went and stayed by the Brook Cherith, which flows into the _____." (2 Kings 17:5)

4. "Then the woman of Zarephath said to Elijah, 'Now by this I know that you are a man of God, and that the word of the LORD in your mouth is _____.'" (2 Kings 4:24)

5. "So he arose and went to _____ . And when he came to the gate of the city, indeed a widow was there gathering _____; and he called to her and said, 'Please bring me a little water in a cup, that I may drink.'" (2 Kings 4:10)

6. "And when the _____ of the man of God arose early and went out, there was an army, surrounding the city with horses and _____." (2 Kings 6:15)

7. "Then Elisha said, 'Hear the word of the LORD. _____ says the LORD: "Tomorrow about this time a seah of fine flour shall be sold for a shekel, and two seahs of barley for a shekel, at the gate of _____."'" (2 Kings 7:1)

8. "So the people _____ out and plundered the tents of the Syrians. So a seah of fine flour was sold for a shekel, and two seahs of barley for a shekel, according to the word of the _____." (2 Kings 7:16)

9. "In the ninth year of Hoshea, the king of Assyria took _____ and carried Israel away to Assyria, and placed them in Halah and by the Habor, the River of Gozan, and in the cities of the _____." (2 Kings 17:6)

10. "They did not obey the voice of the LORD their God, but transgressed His _____ and all that Moses the servant of the LORD had commanded; and they would neither hear nor _____." (2 Kings 18:12)

11. "He removed the high places and broke the sacred _____, cut down the wooden image and broke in pieces the bronze serpent that Moses had made; for until those days the children of Israel burned incense to it, and called it _____." (2 Kings 18:4)

12. "Then Rabshakeh _____ and called out with a loud voice in Hebrew, and spoke, saying, 'Hear the word of the great king, the king of _____!'" (2 Kings 18:28)

13. "And it _____ , as he was telling the king how he had restored the dead to life, that there was the woman whose son he had restored to life, crying out to the king for her house and for her _____." (2 Kings 8:5)

14. "Then he went with _____ the son of
    Ahab to war against Hazael king of
    Syria at Ramoth Gilead; and the
    Syrians wounded _____." (2 Kings
    8:28)

15. "In the twelfth year of Joram the son of
    Ahab, _____ of Israel, Ahaziah the son
    of Jehoram, king of Judah, began to
    _____." (2 Kings 8:25)

16. "So Jehu rode in a chariot and went to
    Jezreel, for _____ lay there. And
    Ahaziah king of Judah had come down
    to see _____." (2 Kings 9:16)

17. "Then he arose and went into the
    house. And he _____ the oil on his
    head, and said to him, 'Thus says the
    LORD God of Israel: "I have anointed
    you king over the people of the LORD,
    over _____."'" (2 Kings 9:6)

18. "And when Jehu had _____ to Jezreel, Jezebel heard of it; and she put paint on her eyes and adorned her head, and looked through a _____." (2 Kings 9:30)

19. "Then they took a bone and spread it under him on the _____ , and they blew the trumpet, and said, 'Jehu is _____!'" (2 Kings 9:13)

20. "And the rest of the acts of Jehoahaz, all that he did, and _____ might, are they not written in the book of the chronicles of the kings of _____?" (2 Kings 13:8)

21. "And Elisha _____ , and they buried him. And the raiding bands from Moab invaded the land in the _____." (2 Kings 13:20)

22. "He restored the _ _ _ _ _ _ of Israel from the entrance of Hamath to the Sea of the Arabah, according to the word of the LORD God of _ _ _ _ _ _ , which He had spoken through His servant _ _ _ _ _ _ ." (2 Kings 14:25)

23. "In the fifteenth year of _ _ _ _ _ _ the son of Joash, king of Judah, Jeroboam the son of Joash, king of Israel, became king in Samaria, and reigned _ _ _ _ _ _ years." (2 Kings 14:23)

24. "And he did evil in the sight of the LORD, but not like his _ _ _ _ _ _ and his mother; for he put away the sacred pillar of Baal that his father had _ _ _ _ _ _ ." (2 Kings 3:2)

25. "Then _____ struck Tiphsah and all who were in it and its territory from Tirzah on; because they did not _____ to him, therefore he struck it. All the women in it who were with child he _____." (2 Kings 15:16)

26. "In the _____ year of Azariah king of Judah, Menahem the son of Gadi became king over Israel, and reigned ten years in _____." (2 Kings 15:17)

27. "And he did what was right in the sight of the LORD, according to all that his _____ Amaziah had done, except that the high places were not removed; the people still sacrificed and burned incense on the _____." (2 Kings 15:34)

28. "In those days the LORD _____ to send Rezin king of Syria and Pekah the son of Remaliah against _____." (2 Kings 15:37)

29. "He did evil in the _____ of the LORD, and walked in the way of Jeroboam and in his sin by which he had made Israel _____." (2 Kings 15:28)

30. "And the rest of the _____ of Pekah, and all that he did, are they not written in the book of the chronicles of the kings of _____?" (2 Kings 15:

Final Thought

As we draw to a close, we must wrap up and remember that the journey through the Bible is not a destination but a continuous adventure. It's a path of discovery, growth, and a deepening relationship with God. As Hebrews 4:12 reminds us, "For the word of God is alive and active." May you experience its vitality, relevance, and transformative power every day.

Thank you for embarking on this journey with us. May the word light your path, guide your steps, and enrich your soul. Pause and reflect on the journey we've undertaken together. The Bible, with its profound wisdom, timeless truths, and life-transforming messages, is not just a book to be read but a relationship to be nurtured, a compass to be followed.

Rizada

LANTERN OF LIFE PUBLISHING

www.lanternoflife.net

Made in the USA
Columbia, SC
14 October 2024

44368498R00067